T0380311

The Race to Redemption

Finish Strong!

Marlaine Peachey

WESTBOW
PRESS®
A DIVISION OF THOMAS NELSON
& ZONDERVAN

WestBow Press books may be ordered through booksellers or by contacting:

WestBow Press
A Division of Thomas Nelson & Zondervan
1663 Liberty Drive
Bloomington, IN 47403
www.westbowpress.com
844-714-3454

ISBN: 979-8-3850-2095-9 (sc)
ISBN: 979-8-3850-2094-2 (e)

Library of Congress Control Number: 2024904710

Print information available on the last page.

WestBow Press rev. date: 03/20/2024

This book is dedicated to my cherished grandchildren,

*Molly, Christian, Katherine, Olivia,
Andrew, Henry & Elaina.*

*You are all by faith, children of God.
My prayer is that you finish strong.*

Contents

ACKNOWLEDGEMENTS

What started out to be a book on "labels", took a new turn upon the revelation of the true reason we are tempted to lose our identity. I have my Father in heaven to thank for that and Him alone. I pray this revelation will touch the hearts of many and give them strength to finish strong.

I want to express sincere gratitude to Carol Fortner, who edited my words, added commas to my life, and encouragement with every turn of the page. You are such a wonderful friend, for whom I shall be eternally grateful.

Finally, I want to thank my loving husband, Marlin, who spent many hours in his favorite chair in the den without me, while I penned away upstairs in my office. Thank you for always believing in me, reading over the final document and giving your undying support. I love you!

Thank you for reading the book! If anyone has questions or comments, feel free to email me at marlaine@currently.com. For a faster response, be sure to put The Race to Redemption in the subject line.

INTRODUCTION

"Yesterday is history, tomorrow is a mystery, today is a gift of God, which is why we call it the present."

Bil Keane

Call me a realist.

When I read through pages of world history, they are not just words of record that were prudently inked on paper. In order to understand and learn what occurred and how it transpired, I mentally engage myself in the scene to experience the incidents. In other words, I get into the story.

In times of war, I can hear the galloping hoofs of horses running to battle. In times of celebration, I can hear the cheers of victory and see the fireworks. In times of struggle, I cringe. My eyes flood at the faces of those experiencing fear and loss of life or family. In times of peace and love, my heart gladdens with joy.

History is vividly filled with events of humanity; true chronicles that spanned over time on this earth. Were it possible, I would love to interview someone from every age and era, uncovering their lifespan of testimonies.

I often wonder how it would have been if I actually lived out my life at those diverse times. What helps me identify with them are the things we have most in common. When they rose in the morning, they saw the same blazing sun that I do and the same shimmering moon at nightfall. When they laid down in the field, or on their rooftops, the stars that sparkled overhead are within the same canopy that I gaze upon with delight and wonder. They tasted food and experienced family and fellowship. Others suffered hardship and trials, knowing little comfort. I, too, have been through tough situations.

But God in His providence has chosen this time for me. I live in a world that has seen knowledge increase. We live at a faster pace because of technology. Although we are far advanced in education and understanding, we still face our own issues. What ties us all together from the very beginning is one continuous ribbon of life progressing through epochs of time that rings true. We are all running the same race. Together we head to the same finish line at a steady pace. Amazingly, it is not a race of time, it's a race to our destiny.

CHAPTER 1

The Race

It seems obvious that the pace we set in this day and age features life in terms of a race. Undoubtedly, it's because most of us never stand still very long - we even call ourselves the human race! In actuality, life is not a fast-paced sprint, it is a continual forward movement, one step at a time, as we head toward our goals in life.

The history we are recording in this age is quite varied. If you could fly across the globe at a low altitude, you would perceive quite a sundry of situations transpiring. Notably, you would witness people starving, versus people flourishing in food production, people at war, people at peace, people in a strong economy, people living in a nation of collapse, people of faith and yes, people of evil. All of this is going on at the same time in different locations.

While the human population is experiencing a plethora of circumstances, we independently focus on our own journey and our own issues. On a personal level, the goals we attempt to attain often have obstacles we must overcome. These hindrances can make us stronger or cause setbacks. As a result, we are constantly going through ups and downs, grasping at strongholds to maintain our balance.

The one common denominator is that we were all created by the same God that formed this world long ago. And while we jog along hurdling our day-to-day schedules, we often fail to recognize there is a spiritual world that is quite busy as well.

We note in Genesis 1, "In the beginning, God created the heavens and the earth." Contrary to derisive opinions, He is not dead, but constantly active in His creation. There are those that acknowledge Him and have connected spiritually; others run their own race. Sadly, there is also an enemy that exists who is more than just an obstacle. He is a cunning disqualifier who would rather see us forfeit the prize than even make it to the finish line.

His aim is to steal, kill and destroy what we set out to accomplish in this marathon of life. In order to stay a step ahead, we need to know his motivation and strategy. Once recognized, it is easy to detect, but requires strength and courage to overtake him in the race. His strategy is not a secret, it's been available to us all along. Most people just don't take the time to discover what they are up against. As a result, their destiny escapes them.

Let's start at the beginning....

CHAPTER 2

The Fall

Long before our time, there was an uprising in heaven. Beauty, power, and pride inspired Satan to believe he could rise to the throne. Amazing to even imagine that anyone could conceive overthrowing God Almighty, there was Lucifer, the Angel of Light, consumed with conceit, planning a coup. His pride must have been on steroids!

In Luke 10, verse 18, Jesus said, "I saw Satan fall like lightning from heaven." Considering the rapid timing of lightning flashes, the defeat must have been a quick blow. Isaiah 14: 12-14 states, "How you are fallen from heaven, O Lucifer, son of the morning....For you have said in your heart, 'I will ascend into heaven, I will exalt my throne above the stars of God......I will ascend above the heights of the clouds, I will be like the Most High God.'"

Ezekiel 28:17 says, "Your heart became proud on account of your beauty, and you corrupted your wisdom because of your splendor. So, I threw you to the earth..." Considering the words of Jesus, he was hurled from heaven. This may be where we get the term "fired." Unfortunately, pride doesn't accept defeat. It is joined by indignation, arrogance, defiance, and rebellion.

One fateful day, as Satan cowered wretchedly in gloom and darkness, the powerful voice of God suddenly emanated throughout the universe, "Let there be light!" And there was light.

What was happening? Would he be reinstated, or could there be a reprieve?

Instead, upon heavenly command, the earth began to take new form. Day after day, the sun, moon, stars, fish, birds, animals, and vegetation appeared. Satan was perplexed. How beautiful everything looked, almost a replica of heaven! And then on the sixth day, God made man. He wasn't greater than Satan, he didn't have the power Satan had been given, but there was one truth of extending evidence that caused jealousy, envy, and hatred to join his company. Adam was made in the image of God. The prince of darkness watched carefully as they walked together in the garden, talking of the man's future. One day he would be heir to all of heaven and sit with Jesus on His throne.

Satan was furious. All of this, in his face! Someone was moving into his territory, walking, and talking with God, and what's this? A woman? Adam had been given everything and his intimacy with God infuriated Satan even more. He planned another take down, this time the very apple of God's eye. Satan was sure of himself; he still had power, and it was greater than this blob of clay. The perfect moment had to take place quickly;

he simply could not bear one more minute of this display of love between God and another being.

The plan was set. Satan knew his situation was due to his own misfortune. By his own foolishness and pride, he forfeited his identity for eternity. And now in hateful revenge, he cunningly planned to steal theirs. God had created everything for their enjoyment and if they fell for dark deceit, they would be Satan's slaves of sin. What's more, by defiling these two prototypes of humanity, every one of their seed would be contaminated.

In Satan's sullied sight, the plan was ingenious.

CHAPTER 3

The Curse

Could it be this easy? Satan marveled at how little effort it took to ruin God's masterpiece. Witnessing the compelling panorama of creation had sickened him, but now with his own supernatural power still intact, he had dealt a fatal blow to humanity. Satan's engagement with the newlyweds took only a few minutes and just that quickly the light had gone out of them.

Welcome to the darkness! He especially fancied the look on their faces when the reality of carnality set in. Everything took on a different appearance. And now their relationship with God was totally severed, just like his. His clever use of deadly duplicity had stolen their position. The perfect man and woman, created in God's image, were now stained with sin. They would be thrown out of the garden just as he had been thrown out of heaven. The revenge was as sweet as the fruit still dripping from their lips. How ridiculous they looked hiding from God, dressed in fig foliage! He could hardly contain heinous laughter as he slithered out of sight to witness God's anger unfold.

Suddenly the eternal booming voice echoed through the garden, "Adam, where are you?"

The author of fear gripped them with a crippling hold and in desperation, their faultfinding fingers pointed to each other, to him, and even to God for the woman He made! Sin knows no shame.

Satan anticipated the sheer joy of seeing them kicked off the planet! It was his territory now, but what came next, he didn't expect. God announced emphatically that there would be enmity between him and the woman. Big deal, he hated her already. She was a useless piece of flesh that cowered quickly, but what is this promise that He would crush his head? Who is HE? It couldn't be Adam; he didn't have that power in his little finger. God declared that man would have to painfully work the soil of cursed ground and the woman would have great pain in childbirth, losing her place as an equal partner. While staggering for them, Satan felt it wasn't the penalty he had experienced.

Something was amiss, but the harbinger of hell knew that God never fails. Although the evil mission was accomplished, a corollary was coming that sounded like his eternal demise.

Satan threw his head back and laughed. "I can ruin this human bloodline until there is no one left to crush my little toe, much less my head. Bring it on! He'll see! Let the games begin!"

CHAPTER 4

The Plan and the Pawn

True to life, the battle has raged on for centuries. After having to regretfully destroy the earth and all the inhabitants by flood except for Noah and family, God made a covenant with Abraham, a man who believed God and trusted in Him. Based on his faith, Abraham, and his descendants, were named His "Chosen People."

Over time, regardless of the miracles of deliverance and provision God bestowed on them, the promise remained but their rectitude was defeated. Judges failed, kings were anointed and annihilated. The people became corrupt and conquered, ending their lives and nation as "idolators." Neighboring empires rose and fell, each one claiming to rule the world, while inward struggles of power and greed broke down their titles of supremacy. Everyone lost their sense of purpose and character.

Finally, the One arrived Who would crush Satan's head. The Father of Lies watched carefully as the Son of God took on the form of a bondservant, bravely leaving the safety of His heavenly home.

"Is this The One who is supposed to crush my head?" he smirked. "His identity will be ruined with pleasure! Let Him try to step on my stage!"

Once the ultimate deceiver was positive this Jesus was "The One and Only" who had come to deliver His people, Satan conceived a plan to end His life quickly, as soon as He was born. Time and again, however, he was foiled. Jesus grew quite popular as a public figure, but who could possibly believe this was God? In the flesh? A mere carpenter and friend of tax collectors and sinners? Really? This foe seemed too easy to terminate.

At first it was touch and go as Jesus escaped temptation and endangerment. But then Satan devised what he thought was a brilliant plot that included the religious ruling council of the day. The hypocritical Pharisees were an easy faction to expend. Supposedly the bearers of God's word, their own conceit and pride made them perfect puppets. They hated the attention Jesus was getting and His identity as Messiah. Although His coming and description were prophesied in scripture, He was not the messiah they wanted. Taking him down would be an easy task. The stage was set, they just had to wait for the right opportunity.

Then, at what he perceived as the right moment, Satan made his move, entered Judas, and personally designed the plan of betrayal. Had Judas paid more attention to the message Jesus gave rather than the money he carried, perhaps he wouldn't have been deceived. Now thanks to a dreadful pretense, the trusted treasurer lost his identity and became the branded "betrayer." After realizing he had succumbed to treachery, Judas could not even bear to live with his declared disloyalty. He ended his life as a pawn of Satan and the damaging label would remain for ages to come.

CHAPTER 5

The Son Rises

The devil and his disciples partied on during the passion, taking every measure to torture and torment The Enemy of Lies. Finally, in a matter of hours, Jesus was publicly punished, and the bloody ordeal was over. The centurion confirmed that He was dead. The earth quaked as the power of hell threw a party that was complete with fireworks.

But then came that glorious Sunday morning when the power of God raised Jesus from death to life, blowing the stone clear off the sealed tomb like a volcanic shock.

Jesus was alive!

Hell erupted into chaos. Satan was sure He was dead. Confusion reigned in the darkness. Jesus never became king on earth. He never took His seat on the temple throne. His life was over and defeated......wasn't it? Something went very wrong. Harrowing to the ears of hell, the proclamation from heaven was a fulfillment of prophecy as far back as the Garden of Eden.

The sins of the world had been paid for in full as the Father accepted Jesus's sacrifice on the cross. No one had been able to pay the heavy debt of the world's sin and without the shedding of blood, there would be no forgiveness. What perfect sacrifice could there be? Did God indeed give Himself? Was Jesus His lamb?

"No! This can't be!" Satan exclaimed.

If only he had realized the true plot, the devil would have never pushed for crucifixion. Satan writhed in disgust. Now, for an eternity he would hate that his ignorance was used in the plan of salvation. It was he that was deceived.

The benefits to Satan's former slaves were more than providential. Jesus had made a way for all believers who trusted and believed in Him to be set free from the slavery and bondage the enemy had held tightly over their heads and around their necks. What's more, His promises were eternal, and they now belonged to the family of God.

What now? The shrewd thief had easily secured their souls and no matter what, he would guard all of hell before giving them up in return. He had seen to it that they had been darkened by sin, and now, those who believed were new creations, completely cleansed by the blood of the lamb! The battle took on new proportions. The sinners had a brand-new identity, the one they were truly created for. All of Satan's work was defeated in one event he proclaimed as victory.

Hosea's prophecy in Chapter 13:14, became suddenly deafening. "I will deliver this people from the power of the grave; I will redeem them from death."

Ouch. This declaration hit hard, but pride comes before a fall.

"This will be a bitter fight till the end," Satan swore. "Surely not everyone will believe. I'll confuse and deceive the masses at every turn. The ones I have, I'll fight hard to keep, but my prize will be the believers. I'll paralyze them in their own faith. I'll create doubt and deception more than ever. This will be my spit in His face! I will never bow to Him!"

CHAPTER 6

Deception

Over 2,000 years have passed, and the cold and callous war between good and evil has undeniably taken on a different front. After all, it was both ruthless and necessary for the enemy to use a new tactic, even though the age-old methods of addiction and sexual immorality gained thousands of vulnerable souls year after year. Evil was clearly recognized in the open field to believers, so the master deceiver cleverly tested a new deception of opposite proportions: hatred and indifference. On the surface, apathy seemed harmless and private to those who believed faith was a personal matter, but it was deeply seated by anger and revenge, tucked away for a later day. As a result, many filed away their spiritual beliefs, and choose to chalk up their misfortunes as "part of life."

Today, victims who are cruelly mistreated by abuse, rape, or rejection, become mentally unstable, losing all capacity to judge or assess their situation in light of what really happened. In the end they suffer from severe depression and contemplate suicide.

These wounded believe that whatever happened to them was either their own fault or even worse, they blame God.

No one considers they live in a fallen world. John 10:10 says, "The thief comes only to steal, kill and destroy, but I came that they may have life and have it to the full."

They woefully cry out, "God where were you?" blaming Him for whatever they endured.

It's not an original thought. Mary and Martha voiced the same complaint to Jesus upon Lazarus's death, "Lord if you had been here, my brother would not have died" (John 11:21).

But Jesus replied "I am the resurrection and the life. The one who believes in Me will live, even though they die, and whoever lives by believing in Me will never die" (John 11:25).

Many believe Jesus' response to Martha applied only to the matter at hand. However, the implication can be applied to other situations. For one, those who are seemingly dead on the inside, can rise in victory over what Satan meant for evil. God promises never to leave us, fail us, nor forsake us (Hebrews 13:5). "And we know that in all things, God works for the good of those who love Him, who have been called according to His purpose (Romans 8:28)."

Instead of temporarily falling from grace, the wounded run away with ears stopped up from any semblance of spirituality. The path to victory entails turning to Him, but instead, they turn their backs in resentment, focusing instead on the damage. The enemy would make us believe our world has ended as we know it, which opens the door to unending fear, bitterness, and anger.

Jesus experienced rejection and shame; however, He trusted His Father and continued in obedience, accomplishing His purpose, paying for the sins of the world. As a result, our Savior is no longer in the tomb and sits in victory at the right hand of God. Believers have His Word that can be trusted implicitly. We can also live on, conquer diversity, and receive eternal life.

CHAPTER 7

The World View

Likewise, on the global scene, humanity has fought back to recover from world wars, pandemics, famine, drought, wildfires, earthquakes, and "natural" weather disasters. Despite the resounding miracles that have occurred, a few brief and forgotten compliments are expressed heavenward, and then astounding accolades are conferred on those who bravely remain. THEY made it through, THEY were restored, THEY are heroes. Within a few months, God is quickly forgotten along with the weak who sadly did not survive.

Year after year, tributes of success are bestowed on those who have invented new strategies, new medicines, and new motivational techniques. They are honored for being the smartest, strongest, and are visionaries of the future.

"We will rebuild!" is the cry of the resilient.

The enemy thrives on this brilliant theory. The work is done mostly by the victims. Those who don't fall in defeat and suffer setback for many years, defiantly rise in pride and are hailed on their riposte to society. God is not needed; they stand in defiance to whatever may come. They are ignorant of its origin and purpose, all the while denying the divine.

As history has often repeated itself, so too, civilizations which were defeated and rebuilt have been recorded unremittingly in various chronicles. Archaeology also tells the tale. In Israel, and elsewhere, there are many "tels" which can easily be seen with the naked eye. They are identified as extremely tall and mountainous flat-top hills, the result of one society being levelled and another rebuilding directly on top, emerging victorious. The process then continues repeatedly until the topmost culture is eventually obliterated.

There is nothing new under the sun, especially when all focus is blinded. It is vitally important to be aware of the two distinct powers on this earth: Almighty God's and a lower, conniving, and contentious enemy, Satan.

The focus to bear is that God is supreme, sovereign, and nothing is impossible for Him. He never fails.

CHAPTER 8

Hidden Motivation and Strategy

Well, there you have it. Satan's hatred of God and His creation will continue until the end of time, but his true motivation is still hidden.

One day, after praying on the subject, I sensed God ask me, "Do you not realize why Satan ultimately wants to ruin my people?"

"Because he hates you, of course," I replied.

"He does hate me, but you must understand the underlying motive. What ultimately drives him on is that ***He lost his position and his identity.*** He wanted to attain My throne, My position, and My identity. He made a grave mistake and lost. There was no way he could go back to his former position, there was no place in heaven for pride, boasting or competition. So, he was thrown out.

"Understand, he totally lost his position and his identity. And now, Satan wants you to lose yours. He wants you to share the misery he experiences with every passing day. And he will stop at nothing to do it. Every dream or vision you had for your future he attempts to taint and torture."

"Take a look around…..sin abounds on the earth; hatred and indifference are resident in every culture and community. It's because people have lost sight of their purpose and reason for life. They are moving in a direction that was not their first agenda."

"Do you think this is the government your forefathers originally envisioned for your country?"

"Did you ever think you would work hard to have a home and family and now you live in a world that is waiting for someone to push a button and annihilate humanity?"

"Or that you would be afraid you could possibly be murdered by an active shooter while shopping for groceries?"

"Did you ever imagine that your children would be questioned to choose their gender when I have formed them in their mother's womb? Others are snuffed out before they have a chance to gasp for breath."

"I carefully design and give life in the womb and humanity foolishly chooses to end it when they are tempted with selfishness, thinking it will set them free; instead, they become slaves of sin. In My face, Satan sees that those innocent lives are dismembered and discarded. But I have them. I will not lose one the Father has given Me. Each one is a treasure to Me."

"Now you know his motive and strategy: to steal everyone's identity on this earth and take them down because that was his own demise."

My mind was staggering. I had to sit and take that in for a moment. I had never contemplated such a scheme before, but now the truth burned in my heart.

I understand now, how we can be toyed with as pawns until we meet Jesus, and how much Satan relishes our downfalls. Only a miserable loser could be such an underhanded, hateful, devious enemy! It has often been said, "Misery loves company." No wonder he wants to take as many with him as he can. He drives our train of thoughts, hurts and happenstances to run rampant and throw us totally off track.

Only truth can derail that train. The good news is, Truth is a person.

CHAPTER 9

We Have Been Made Worthy

One of the biggest hindrances we face is unworthiness. The enemy will not only tie you down with that lie, but he will also drill it into your brain repeatedly, until you firmly believe it. Satan's modus operandi is to beguile you (just like he did Eve) and use a little veracity totally out of context. Jesus called him the Father of Lies.

Whatever you have been through, or are even facing now, your mind may be insisting one of the following is true:

1. This is your fault.
2. You made a mistake.
3. You are the problem.
4. Your life is over.
5. You are not worthy of getting past what has happened.

You can be sure those thoughts are coming from your worst enemy. His goal is to make you believe your back is against the wall, and you are abandoned, with no way out in sight,

Satan's half-truth is an attempt to do you in, because:

1. He hates God and enjoys bringing down his creation.
2. Controlling your mind is the easiest way to keep you in bondage.
3. He cares nothing about you and hates the fact that even in your lost state, you reflect the image of God.
4. He wants more than anything to bring you down to his level.
5. He wants radical revenge for losing his own identity.

Scripture does say because of sin we are unworthy. Romans 3:10 states, "There is no one righteous, not even one; there is no one who understands; there is no one who seeks God. All have turned away, they have together become worthless; there is no one who does good, not even one."

But that's not the whole truth. God, who made us in His image, loves us more than we can ever realize. He knew the temptations would be strong and, because of our sinful nature, we would fall. So, before He ever said, "Let there be light," He planned to rescue us. He ordained that without the shedding of blood there would be no forgiveness of sins. In order for us to be free, someone had to pay. Sin could never exist in heaven. God also said no man could ever ransom his own soul. God's only choice was to pay the price Himself.

Because of His love for us, He sent His Son, not because we deserved it, not because we are good people, or resemble Him, or try hard. *God did it because we first belonged to Him.* And it was the only way He could get us back.

The Father wanted us to live with him for eternity; the choice, however, is ours. God created us with free will so we could freely choose. He doesn't want anyone to perish. He doesn't "send" anyone to hell. That choice is our own.

Do we choose Him, or the enemy? That seems like a preposterous question. Who in their right mind wouldn't accept God as their choice? Who would choose hell for eternity? The answer is, only those whose minds have been totally deceived.

God offers us the whole truth: "For all have sinned and fall short of the glory of God, and ***all are justified freely by His grace through the redemption that came by Christ Jesus" (Romans 3:23).*** And again, "For the wages of sin is death ***but the free gift of God is eternal life in Christ Jesus our Lord"*** (Romans 6:23). And finally, 2 Corinthians 5:21, "God made Him who had no sin to be sin for us, so that ***in Him we might become the righteousness of God."***

CHAPTER 10

Our True Identity

When we accept Christ as our Savior, our identity changes from being a slave of sin to being a child of God and heir of heaven. John 1:12 says, "For as many as received Him, to them He gave the power to become children of God."

The enemy would have you believe that we are all children of God, and we have all been abandoned to the perilous pitfalls of life, which falsely frames God as a sorry, unfair, unloving Father.

The truth is we are all sinners and do not become children of God until we make that choice in faith, believing and trusting in Him.

Have you ever formally accepted Him? If you do indeed believe in Him and what He did for you, today you can become His child. You can accept Him in your own words, or say this simple prayer, providing you mean it in your heart.

"God, I believe in You. I believe Jesus was your Son Who came to die for my sins and rose from the dead. I am asking forgiveness for the sins I have committed. Please come into my heart and be my Savior and Lord. I will follow You all the days of my life. Thank You for Your gift of eternal life. In Jesus name I pray, Amen."

The Bible says that now you are a new creation, and even the angels are rejoicing in heaven over your decision. Before now, you were lost in a fallen world. Now because of your faith in what He did for you, you belong to Him. The Apostle Peter wrote in 1 Peter 1:3, "Praise be to the God and Father of our Lord Jesus Christ! In his great mercy he has given us new birth into a living hope through the resurrection of Jesus Christ from the dead." You now have the privilege of a personal relationship with the God who made you, saved you, and will be living in your heart from this point on.

The good news is that your current circumstances may not immediately change but He will deliver you to a new position in life if you trust in Him. And, "...being confident of this, that He Who began a good work in you will carry it on to completion until the day of Christ Jesus" (Philippians 1:6).

Remember, you don't have an indigent defender on your side. You have the Creator of the universe as your advocate, Who has received you as His own. He is now your provider, protector, and refuge. Be aware that Satan will surely tell you that you are not God's child.

God does not lie. He says, "Do not fear, I have redeemed you; I have summoned you by name; you are mine" (Isaiah 43:1).

CHAPTER 11

God is Our Protection

When you become a child of God, or perhaps you have been for some time, it is important that you grow strong.

You must stand steady on your feet. God is living in you; it doesn't mean you lie down and let the world run over you. You have gained an important position and God loves you. He wants you to grow spiritually into a robust reflection of Him and the masterfully designed creation He made. Your physical body may have taken on years of wear, but your spirit can maintain a youthful resiliency, preparing you for eternal life with Him.

According to the Book of Ephesians, the Apostle Paul tells us we have been given a spiritual armor to fight not physical, but heavenly battles. As mentioned before, just because we are now children of God doesn't mean we are immune to the wiles of Satan; we are, however, by His authority, fortified with defense. As we maintain that composure, we are victors. No encounter with the enemy is ever won if someone lays aside their armor. The battle is The Lord's, but we have been given protection that is necessary to identify and exercise.

In order to stand, we must have strong legs, that's why the scripture says our loins should be girded with truth. When we acquire truth, we can solidly stand and not falter.

It is crucial to know who we are as children of God and not let any doubts confuse us. Scripture says we should wear our helmet of salvation; head gear that protects our minds from lies.

God knows our hearts are tender and can quickly become bitter with loss and revenge. He has given us a breastplate of righteousness to protect the center of our sensitivity.

We need to move forward in our faith, gaining ground in our growth, not retreating in flight. We have been given "gospel shoes" to walk firmly in the message of salvation, always sure of the gift we have been given by the shed blood of our Savior. Physically our feet can be painfully stressed in many ways, but spiritually these shoes protect us with the peace that passes understanding.

God lives in us and has given us a shield to protect us from attack. That shield is faith and must not be thin skinned. During the days of the Roman empire, battalions carried heavy shields for protection. Some were as long as their body, but they could withstand attack, even from fiery darts. Our spiritual shields are not heavy to carry but must have a measure of depth to resist the enemy. Faith can be fortified by truth and strong convictions of who our God is. When we are solidly armored, we can be hit with more than flaming darts; cannonballs may be diverted, if our faith is built upon truth and salvation.

The weapon we have been issued is our sword. It is the same one Jesus used in the wilderness, the Word of God. It is truth, which confounds lies. It is formidable, because it is flawless and dominant over the enemy who stands on the liability of lies. The double-edged sword of truth divides apart fact and fiction, certainty and uncertainty, reality and falsehood, integrity and evil.

With this armor, we have been given protection from attack, and yet while conceptual in thought, these pieces of armor are actually God Himself. He is our salvation, He is our righteousness, He is our peace, He is our shield, He is truth, and His Word is our weapon. John states in his gospel, "The Word was God." God Himself is our protection and He cannot fail.

CHAPTER 12

Training for Triumph

The word "athlete" is derived from the Greek and means "contestant in the games." In ancient times, anyone could sign up for an Olympic event, but the term was usually reserved for those who had been highly trained to compete, showing dedication, skill, and fitness to participate.

As a child of God in the race to redemption, you are set apart, but you must be fit to finish. Having the right attire will keep you from stumbling but will not give you the stamina to compete with endurance. You must be trained.

Everything you need to know God has written for you in a manual, called the Bible. We read in 2 Timothy 3: 16 – 17, "All Scripture is God-breathed and is useful for teaching, rebuking, correcting and training in righteousness."

Those who follow the guise of religion will find themselves far off track from the truth. A participant must be in physical shape to finish, but in this race, it is imperative that you feed your spirit. As Jesus said in John 6:63, "The spirit gives life, the flesh counts for nothing."

If you are to continue with vigor, reading the Word of God will strengthen your spirit as well as your heart, giving you wisdom and discernment at every turn. His Word also gives continuous revelation of Him, Who is Truth. The more you read, the more He reveals Himself to you. There is not one training manual on this earth that can offer the same benefit.

The One who made you saw to it that His very Word was available to you as a manual to live; therefore, laying it aside and running your own race is futile. If you think about it, our bodies have been masterfully designed; the entire universe is beyond our understanding and comprehension. If indeed there is a manual that has been given to us to follow, with directions for safety to employ in this life, who would want to ignore it or live without it? The wisdom and instruction of a master creator is both necessary and vital in our world. Thankfully, our loving Father did not abandon us to figure it out on our own. He provided instructions to live by. Paul said in 1 Corinthians 9, "Everyone who competes in the games goes into strict training.....therefore I do not run like someone running aimlessly; I do not fight like a boxer beating the air." He also states in Colossians 2:7, "We need to be rooted and built up in Him, strengthened in the faith." The bottom line is that reading the Bible gives you knowledge but putting it into practice empowers your life. That's how you finish strong.

Chapter 13

Position vs. Identity

The enemy uses various tactics against us, but they generally fall under three categories:

1. Change of position.
2. Labeling.
3. An attempt to steal your true identity.

While the enemy knows all three must be successful, these tactics build upon one another and play a necessary part in cutting you off as you approach the finish line. This is where your identity comes in, and the disqualifier will try to move in for the defeat. You must remember who you are, Who your protector is, and stand firm.

Unfortunately, people take great pride in their positions in life and mistakenly treat their position as their identity. When they completely believe their status is who they are in life, no matter how great or small, and that position changes, the takedown can be great.

In life, if that position were placed on a pedestal, the change can be so paramount that the victim cannot imagine God could possibly move them on to something better. Even worse, if they have been in that position for a while, they may believe they have arrived on their own laurels and God had nothing to do with it. They either collapse because they cannot accept failure, or if they attribute their success to God and it changed, it's His fault that it was lost. He must have abandoned them.

Most of the time, not always, this involves a change physically, whether internal or external. The blame game will begin; chaos, offense and hatred will take residence and the trap door quickly closes. As soon as the change of position has been secured, Satan quickly moves forward with the second category, "labels."

Chapter 14

Labels: The Earmarks of Slavery

Have you ever worn a new blouse or shirt and the label on the back of the collar was totally irritating? The uncomfortable agitation will drive you out of your mind until it is removed. If scissors are not readily available, you might be tempted to tear it off, but if it is an expensive shirt or delicate material, you could chance ruining it forever.

In life, an event can occur that brings with it a blistering label. The incident may be traumatic, such as rape, divorce, widowhood, abortion or abuse and the label that Satan firmly attaches can make your life miserable. No scissors can remove the stigma and although you keep it close to you and hidden in secret, you may be way too sensitive to deal with it in the open and thus, you are consigned to let it remain, sometimes for a lifetime.

There are people walking around this earth today who have been indelibly marked by such labels which cannot be seen by the naked eye, but deep inside they carry the maddening truth.

Few of us have escaped this method of being mentally cut off in the race of life. The label can be as simple as "fat," "uncoordinated," or even "ignorant." But to the person who is hurt, the pain runs deep. Satan wants to "score" us as victims of his work to inhibit our full deliverance and the furtherance of the gospel. If we should experience divorce, bankruptcy, health issues, widowhood, rape and so on, the enemy looms these claims over us to make us believe that because we have lost our position, we are forever doomed to live under those damaging designations.

These earmarks of slavery must be eradicated for us to move on in life, otherwise they could be used another day to bring us to defeat.

"So, if the Son sets you free, you are free indeed" (John 8:36). "For He has rescued us from the dominion of darkness and brought us into the kingdom of The Son He loves, in Whom we have redemption, the forgiveness of sins" (Colossians 1:13).

CHAPTER 15

The Sheep and the Goats

You might be thinking, if I lost my position and were living with dreadful labels what more can I lose? Isn't that my whole identity?

As mentioned before, your identity is not your position, nor are the labels that have been put on you. Your identity is who you really are. You were created for one purpose, to spend eternity with your Creator. It doesn't matter if you are a banker, politician, police chief, doctor, teacher, janitor, clerk, or stay at home mom (which is a real and important job); your identity is found in Him. Either you are one of His or you are not; it has been your choice all along. He has done everything possible to give you the identity of being a child of God and heir of heaven. That choice is gained by total trust and surrender to His care.

Jesus said in the end he will separate the sheep from the goats. One way or the other, we will all be a part of that discretion. Don't let the wool fool you. Sheep aren't that smart. They leave the flock and run off, they may eat poison berries, drink polluted water, or even become cast, which is when they are helpless on their backs and can't revert on their feet alone. But they have one thing in common; they know their Shepherd. They rely on His guidance. They know His love for them and have lived under his care since He was made their owner. They belong to Him, and they know His voice. So, if that is your identity, don't let the wool be pulled over your eyes. Be aware of being deceived no matter how green the other pasture looks. Who would willingly join a bunch of head-butting goats? You have been bought with the precious blood of Jesus Christ. Never forget that.

The tactics I have mentioned don't come as little slaps on the hand. The enemy comes to steal, kill, and destroy. If you don't know who your God is and who you are, you will believe anything.

The proof is in the Bible. God made a covenant with Abraham that His descendants would be His people. God kept that covenant, but they decidedly chose otherwise. When He delivered them from Egypt, instead of being thankful, they grumbled, made a golden calf, and were embittered at their deliverance. They refused to believe God would give them the promised land and allow them to conquer the people in it. They wanted to go back to Egypt. They would rather be in bondage as slaves! As a result, God let them wander for 40 years until all the adults died, save Joshua and Caleb who chose to believe God.

Later in the Old Testament, God blessed them with homes they didn't build and vineyards they didn't grow. The country expanded under Solomon and the world knew there was a God in Israel. But along with wealth and possessions, they began to worship false gods. No matter what prophet came and warned them of destruction, they insisted on the worship of their choice and spurned Almighty God. It wasn't a one-night stand. They continued for years worshiping Baal, who was of course, demonic. Is it any wonder that they were conquered and destroyed? The north was vanquished by the barbaric Assyrians and the south exiled to Babylon. None of the elders who left at an old age saw their land again. Seventy years later the remnant began to return but many chose to stay in Persia!

Years later, they found themselves under Roman oppression. Once again, they were destroyed in 70 A.D. Those who escaped remained in the diaspora until World War II. At that time Satan attempted to destroy them completely, but God had a plan, and He led them home. Since 1948 they are still returning, as was prophesied. But now it is a struggle to once again live in the land God originally gave to them. If only they had stayed faithful in the past. God is not only calling them home, He is calling them to Him.

This is a lesson for all of us. God calls us to be His own, but we have a choice. It's hard to believe, but people of every nation turn to their own devices and reject God altogether. And those who do, will continue to the bitter end. When God's wrath is poured out, nonbelievers won't even beg for forgiveness. The Bible says they will shake their fists and gnash their teeth at Him. I can't even imagine…

CHAPTER 16

Repentance vs. Remorse

God did not send His Son to die for the sins of the world and extend eternal life to those who would throw it back in His face.

In John 6: 47 Jesus says, "Truly, truly I say to you, he who believes has eternal life." That word belief as it was written in the Greek is to totally trust and surrender.

He never said, "No matter what you think, heaven is for you! I will take you kicking and screaming into paradise."

God is not unfair, and He will go to the ends of the earth and beyond to draw you to Him, but He will not force you. He is fully aware that backsliding will occur because you will be deceived and tempted. He experienced those temptations Himself. Backsliding will not remove you from His love; repentance restores you to complete fellowship. Separation from God is when you turn your back on Him, claiming in full recognition and deliberation your decision to go against Him.

Peter betrayed Jesus and so did Judas. Peter repented and wept bitterly. Despite having been given the power to heal the sick and raise the dead when they went out two by two, Judas wanted it done His way. He had experienced the power and the person of Jesus and knew exactly what He was doing. It was his choice.

When I first accepted Christ as my Savior, I knew that I had been forgiven for things I had done wrong. I wondered why Satan had sinned only once, (however big of course) and could never be forgiven. I actually felt sorry for him when I realized how much I had done. That's when I learned he did not want to be forgiven. ***Repentance is not in his vocabulary, revenge is.*** He is not sorry; he is adamant that his way be done, and he will take everyone that he can with him. From his sick perspective, even if he burns in hell forever, he rejoices that he won over some of God's creation, the ones Jesus died for and paid for with His blood.

If Satan can take you that far, far enough to totally reject Christ for eternity, after you knew Him well, and you want no part in Him, then the enemy has stolen your identity and the race to your destiny is over.

Additional note: If that concerns you, it is evident you haven't gone to the other side, you just need to draw near and follow The Lord. If that doesn't concern you at all, you are either sure of your identity in Christ, or you are sure that is not the way you want to go. You are free to choose.

Chapter 17

Will You Stand in Faith?

So, let's get back on track. If you know who you are in Christ, you are probably growing in your relationship with Him. You may have a strong faith and thank God every day for what He has done for you. But how long will your faith hold up in troubled times? Can you still believe God in times of war, times of tragedy, times of personal loss, times of danger?

There is no need to worry or live in fear. If you are a child of God, you know where you are headed, come what may. Hebrews 12:2 says, "...for the joy set before Him, He endured the cross, scorning its shame, and sat down at the right hand of the throne of God."

In other words, although Jesus was being mocked, spit upon, constantly hit on the head, crowned with thorns, and crucified, He did not consider the shame that He endured. His eyes were fixed on the prize, and He knew the joy was coming. Jesus was sure of it. There was nothing that would deter Him from paying the price. That is the love God has for us.

Could you do that for your kids? No matter how much you love them, it would be pretty hard to think, "We'll all be in heaven one day!" while you were dying on a cross. I admit the pain would be overbearing and no matter how much I love my kids, if I had to die for them, I would, but joy wouldn't be in my thoughts. I would be crying like a baby.

Times are getting tougher you have to admit, and according to scripture, one day they will be much worse. Some maintain that we will never see those days as Christians; if that is true, sign me up! However, after studying the scriptures, I am sure we will not go through the wrath of God, but that's not to say we won't see some pretty tough times.

Could you make it through? I'm not talking about food storage, a bomb shelter, and enough ammo to annihilate a small country. I'm talking about not denying Christ. Would you be able to stand no matter what the condition?

When I first got saved, I led my children to the Lord and explained to them that if such a day ever came, and their lives were threatened, never deny Him. The next minute you will be in heaven anyway. Today they are married with their own kids and have never forgotten it. I wanted to make sure they would never turn back. I pray you don't either. God never turned back on your salvation and willingly paid the price for you.

"Therefore, He is able to save completely those who come to God through Him, because He always lives to intercede for them" (Hebrews 7:25).

We serve a loving, faithful God. Never give up! Remember, no matter what you face here, joy is before you.

CHAPTER 18

No Fear in Love

So now we keep the pace, and live our best lives, knowing God has a plan. Each of us is part of His body, the church. His plan is that we enjoy our relationship with Him, not follow the pretext of religion. We are privileged to have a personal relationship with the Creator of the universe!

For now, we have work to do. Not works that will get us to heaven, Jesus did the one thing that will get us there. I'm referring to the work that God wants to do through us. There is no mistaking it. You were born with a purpose. You were not an accident, no matter what you were told. You are unique, one of a kind and you have a place in this universe.

Some feel ill equipped to do a job they were meant to do or can't imagine getting it done. If that is your case, you are right where you are supposed to be. When God assigns you a task, He will equip you and there is no pressure on doing it alone. Jesus said in John 15:5, "Apart from Me, you can do nothing."

God's work can never be achieved on your own strength; He desires to invite you to be His vessel.

Moses experienced this first hand. God asked him to lead over 2 million people out of Egypt. He threw up several excuses of being inept and impossible to task. But God did mighty miracles as Moses yielded and obeyed.

The fact that you are still breathing means your work is not complete. You will never fulfill your true meaning or experience a situation that God chose for you to accomplish, if you give up on life. Giving up is hopelessly dismal, when being strong, courageous and obedient will enable you to see God Himself at work, even in your weakness. Nothing is impossible with God nor is His hand short that it cannot save. It is incredibly exciting and victorious to witness great and mighty miracles done by the hand of God that only He can do.

CHAPTER 19

Path, Purpose & Privilege

In this "human race" we all have a path to take, a purpose to live and a privilege to experience this life. When you choose God,

1. The path you take will be illuminated by His Word.
2. Your purpose will drive you toward your destiny and your destiny to your destination.
3. You will be given the privilege to experience not just a world of amazing discoveries, but also the opportunity to be a child of the very One Who created the universe and you.

He is not a "life coach" as we know on earth. As you grow in your relationship with Him, you will learn that He knows every hair on your head and cares more about you than you do yourself. Every breath you take, every step you make, begins with Him, ends with Him and is ordained by Him when you are His. No matter how hard you have fallen, God desires to rescue you and return you to His arms. As a parent sees his own features in the face of his child, so God sees His image in us and knows His own. He longs to spend eternity with you and me, and what He has planned for us, we cannot even imagine!

"Therefore, since we are surrounded by such a great cloud of witnesses, let us throw off everything that hinders and the sin that so easily entangles. And let us run with perseverance the race marked out for us, fixing our eyes on Jesus, the pioneer and perfecter of faith" (Hebrews 12:1-2).

AFTERWORD

My purpose in writing this book is to help people realize their value and purpose in this world, the opportunity they have been given, the free choice that has been bestowed on them, and how much they are loved by God.

We all experience battles in life, but God will never forsake us. If you understand your enemy's true motive, there should be no cause to ever fear anyone or anything, because we belong to a loving, compassionate, and merciful Father. The same loving God who provided His own Son to pay the price for our sins so we could have eternal life. A God Who never fails.

For now, stay on track, and keep your eyes on the goal. Finish strong!

About the Author

Marlaine Peachey was born and raised in New Orleans, Louisiana, and attended Loyola University. She accepted the Lord in 1977, converting to Christianity after being raised for 27 years in a religion that offered no assurance of salvation nor personal relationship with God. Since that time, she has shared the joy of her testimony at luncheons, dinners, churches and conferences across the south. For over 15 years she trained inspirational speakers, and for the past 45 years has taught bible studies to women of all ages. She travels yearly, leading tours to Israel and attended Israel College of the Bible in Jerusalem where she studied archaeology.

During this time, she also served for 20 years as the Mayor's Executive Assistant in Mandeville, Louisiana, (now retired), and appears at various professional conferences as a motivational and educational speaker in her field. Today, Marlaine is an author, journalist, editor, seasoned speaker and writing consultant.

For more information with any of the above, or to book Marlaine for tours or speaking engagements, call (985) 630-1798 or email her at marlaine@currently.com.

NOTES

Other books written by or collaborated with Marlaine Peachey

Sharing the gospel in today's world may seem a daunting task to some, but when you take a closer look at whose job it really is and what needs to be said, the burden is lifted and the commission becomes an adventure. This study will guide you to simplify your words, study the truth, learn how to be led by the Spirit, know and understand those you meet, engage them to discipleship, make yourself available to Christ, and embark on the assignment set before you.

At this very moment, there are people yet unsaved who are longing and eager to fill the emptiness in their hearts. If you are a willing vessel, God will use your love story to change their lives forever.

Available at Christian bookstoes, Amazon, Barnes & Nobles, or Westbowpress.com. For more books, search Marlaine Peachey online.

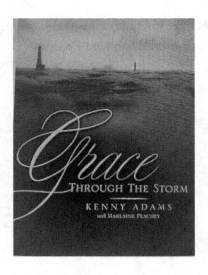

Kenny Adams operates his construction business on spiritual principles the Lord has taught him on the job. In Grace Through the Storm, Kenny explains "Using the tools of the trade." "The Lord has turned me from struggling to prospering - because I started doing what He wanted me to do, not what I thought I should do."

"As a result, the journey is tremendously fulfilling and a lot less complicated. The Lord gave me these principles: Be obedient and give Me the glory. Seek Ye first the kingdom of God and His righteousness. His grace is sufficient."

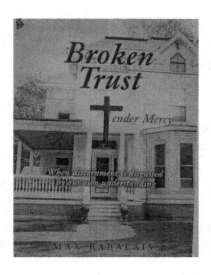

Vivid dreams can occur on any given night, but the American dream takes a lifetime. Allen took hold of his vision and gave life the best he had, working to capacity, reaching for the stars, and chasing his goal.

But as life's journey often takes detours, Allen soon found himself on unfamiliar ground. He had lost his way and hope began to crumble. The only way home was to learn Who to trust and where to place his faith.

Printed in the United States
by Baker & Taylor Publisher Services